I Stood on a Knoll South of Norton

BY ELDON ARCHER

◆ FriesenPress

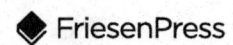

Suite 300 - 990 Fort St
Victoria, BC, V8V 3K2
Canada

www.friesenpress.com

Copyright © 2016 by Eldon Archer
First Edition — 2016

All rights reserved.

No part of this publication may be reproduced in any form, or by any means, electronic or mechanical, including photocopying, recording, or any information browsing, storage, or retrieval system, without permission in writing from FriesenPress.

ISBN
978-1-4602-8786-6 (Hardcover)
978-1-4602-8787-3 (Paperback)
978-1-4602-8788-0 (eBook)

1. BIOGRAPHY & AUTOBIOGRAPHY, PERSONAL MEMOIRS

Distributed to the trade by The Ingram Book Company

Clyde Archer

Susie Archer

❧ Hazel and Eldon ❦

❧ *Emaline & Cora* ☙

I STOOD ON A KNOLL SOUTH OF NORTON, SEARCHING my soul, as to why I was here. For more than a year, I had a reoccurring urgency to return to the land of my youth. The emotions were strong and I thought that maybe this nagging was because I was overdue in visiting my Mother and Father's graves. As I looked out over the valley formed by the Prairie Dog creek, I knew that the feelings, stirring within me, were more than that. For sometime, I have had the feeling that the clock of my life was nearing four thirty in the afternoon. I seemed to be spending more time reminiscing about the good fortunes of my life and the people who had contributed to them. The movies of my mind were continually bringing up people, time, places, and events, shelved in the recesses of my mind for so many years.

Why do impulses come and go? Some we act upon, others we do not. To conjecture, more than likely, would lead to more questions than answers.

I STOOD ON A KNOLL SOUTH OF NORTON, ankle deep in buffalo grass that during the starlight-hours of night, had been, ever so gently, sprinkled by the dew fairy. Surveying the landscape through heavy moist air, gently illuminated in the early light of dawn, I was viewing the land where my life began. It all started here. The here and now were blending with my memory of happy times of my youth. Tears swelled in my eyes, and my nose tingled, as I stood there with goose bumps running down my back. It was time again to give God in heaven thanks for his great generosities. Whether by luck or by God's plan I have been blessed all of my life? Thank you God, for choosing my parents with such great care.

I STOOD ON A KNOLL SOUTH OF NORTON reviewing the memory-movies of days long ago, yet so clear that it could have been yesterday. Clyde and Susie Archer, names well known in Norton County, made a decision in the spring of 1930 to move from Norton to a small farm on the south bank of the Prairie Dog creek. To them it offered the best of both worlds since it was only a mile and a half from town.

Even though I was only four, I remember the spring day of our moving from the little two-bedroom house in the south part of Norton to this little farm. What an exciting place for a four year old!

Some people might think that twelve acres hardly constitutes a farm, but it offered everything that my parents had experienced in their youth, plus we had three acres of timber and a creek with deep, clear, swimming holes. Cane pole fishing for bullheads, and blue gills was only a hundred yards from the house. Large, mature, cottonwood trees surrounded our house offering shade and a home to a family of squirrels.

The house was huge compared to the one we had moved from. The dinning room and living room together were as large as the whole house in Norton. Two big pocket doors could be pulled out of the walls to close off the living room. This was especially handy in the winter, as we did not have to heat the living room unless we were expecting company. Adjoining the large kitchen where we ate most of our meals there was a large walk in pantry with shelves along one wall and a worktable with a sink attached to the other wall. A west window looked out on the side yard making this big pantry open and comfortable. A large sink had been installed in the workbench. There was no plumbing in the house so any water poured into the sink drained through a pipe that went through the outside wall and into large wooden rain barrel.

Our drinking water was carried from the well to the house in a two gallon galvanized pail and we used a community dipper to ladle out water over vegetables being cleaned in the sink or for a fresh drink of water. After each meal we used a second pail to carry water in from the well to heat in two dishpans on the stove, one for washing and the other for rinsing. Washing and drying the dishes after each meal were chores allotted to siblings.

Each morning and evening the pantry was used to separate the cream from the whole milk in our cream separator also attached to the worktable. On top of our cream separator was a large stainless steel bowl to hold the milk that Dad brought from the barn to the house. A cream separator is actually a big centrifuge. Two spouts, one for cream, the other for separated milk, surrounded a cone shaped cylinder that performed the separation. By turning a large crank the cone shaped cylinder started spinning and when the right speed had been reached Dad turned on the spigot at the bottom of the big bowl and the milk flowed into the center of the spinning cone. Cream being lighter was thrown toward one spout while the heavier separated milk flowed to the other.

It was a tricky procedure because the speed was critical. Many times for one reason or another I have seen milk all over the table and floor. This was accompanied by fault finding between my parents. A far less efficient method was to let the milk sit and the cream would rise to the top and then it could be skimmed off. Pasteurizing was an unknown word in Norton. Even the milk delivered by the milkman to people's homes in Norton, was raw milk. Many of the milk bottles had a bulge in the neck where the cream colleted after separating from the milk. The cream was carefully poured off into a cream pitcher to be used in coffee or on the morning's portion of porridge.

There were so many new things for my sister and I who were born in town but old hat to my parents born on farms.

AT TWILIGHT, THE CRICKETS BEGAN TO SING THEIR evening serenade and after all the evening chores were done our family often sat on the big front porch to enjoy the end of a country day. We watched jackrabbits and cottontails creep from their hiding places and move into the neighbor's alfalfa field that was just across the road. There, they could nibble away undisturbed until first light of dawn.

THE BARN HAD FOUR STALLS, TO ACCOMMODATE ANY milk cows and horses that with time and money my folks would purchase. The haymow in the top half of the barn, could hold a winter's supply of alfalfa hay to be fed to any livestock that we might own.

There was a chicken house, not big, but adequate, especially when you have not had time to buy any laying hens. The windmill tower was made of wood, but the shiny galvanized metal of the windmill head, looked new. There are certain sounds that time or age can never erase. One of those sounds is the music of a windmill as the wind turns the big blades furnishing the power to pull water from deep within the earth. It is so quiet here on this knoll before sunrise, but within my head, I can hear the music of the mill and I can see in my mind's eye the flow of cold, crystal-clear, water flowing into the stock tank.

It was an idyllic place for a boy like me to grow up, but it was a big challenge for my parents. We were leaving the conveniences of electric lights, running water, and an inside toilet, for: light by oil lamp, water at a windmill a hundred feet from the house, and a two-hole outhouse.

The Norton light plant was over a half a mile from our house and it was two years or more before my parents saved enough money to pay for and install power lines from the light plant to our house. The magic of electricity eliminated many hardships. No longer would we hear the hiss of the Coleman lamp hanging from the kitchen ceiling as the glowing mantels held back the darkness. Retiring our oil lamps eliminated several chores. There were no wicks to trim, no chimney globes to polish, and the odor of kerosene, no longer tainted the air. Switching on a light as one entered a dark room eliminated the carrying of an oil lamp and the accompanying danger of fire.

As soon as Dad wired the house for the electrical current to flow to the outlets, he installed an electric pump-jack at the windmill. No longer would we have to depend upon the wind to turn the mill or to pump water by hand on windless days.

I can remember my dad insisting on buying my mother an electric washing machine, so she could retire her washboard and clothes stopper. This washing machine was a mechanical marvel to a six-year-old and a back saver to my mother. It looked like half of a wooden barrel on skinny iron legs. The sides, bottom, and lid had been fashioned from one-inch thick oak staves. The hinged wooden lid had a steel shaft extending through it. Under the lid, attached to this shaft, was the dasher. The dasher was fashioned from a thick piece of circular wood pierced by four, one-inch thick wooden dowels about five inches long and rounded on the ends. With the lid closed, the dowels extended down into the clothes being washed in the hot sudsy water. The dasher swished the clothes back and forth through the water releasing the soil and grime from the clothes

The power to activate the dasher was an electric motor with a large steel wheel connected to the motor shaft. Attached at the outer edge of the wheel was a push rod resulting in a cam-wheel action. As the wheel turned, the pushrod moved back and forth which in turned activated a vertical walking-arm. This walking-arm was attached to the outside of the tub at a center pivot point. At the top of the walking arm, was a clevis hinge that connected to a bar of steel with vertical grooves. The grooves meshed into the cogwheel of the dasher shaft. As the cam wheel turned, the walking arm pushed and pulled the bar of steel meshed to the dasher shaft and generated the, to and fro, action of the dasher.

It sounds like a Rube Goldberg innovation, but it sure beat scrubbing clothes by hand on a metal washboard.

Today this washing machine would be an OSHA nightmare. In fact, there would be no way that a manufacture could offer it for sale because there was so many ways one could get hurt. Everything was exposed. Clothing, hair, and fingers were ready targets for all of the many moving parts.

Housewives, as they were called in those days, had a specific day for specific chores. Everyone had embroidered tea towels with Monday designated as washday. I looked forward to washday, because I would get to help my Mom. When she decided that the clothes had washed long enough to be clean, it was my job to run the clothes through the wringer. I would stand on a kitchen chair and fish the washed clothes out of the hot soapy water with a wash stick. This was a one-inch dowel about three feet long. It was very important that I push the wet clothes up to the wringer with the stick where the two rubber rollers of the wringer could grab the clothes and squeezed the soapy water out of them before they dropped into the first washtub of hot rinse water.

Occasionally the rollers would catch the stick and it too, went through with the clothes. I clearly remember the many horror-stories my Mother told me about women getting their hair or hand caught in the wringer rollers. The point of these stories was to impress upon me the importance of safety.

After the clothes went through the wringer rollers that squeezed out most of the soapy wash water my mother would put in the next batch of dirty clothes for washing.

My next duty was to slosh the clothes up and down in the warm rinse water to get most of the soap out of them. When Mother was satisfied that I had done a good job, she would adjust the wringer so that I could wring the clothes from the first rinse water into the second washtub full of cool bluing rinse water. Liquid bluing was added to the rinse water to make white clothes look whiter. After a few minutes in the bluing water, I sent the clothes through the wringers for the third and final time. The clothes dropped into the clothes-basket ready for hanging outside on the clothesline.

Washday was exactly that. It took most of the day. It was necessary to carry about thirty gallons of water from the well to the kitchen. My Mother used a wash boiler on top of the wood stove to heat the wash water and the first rinse water. She added lye to the water while it was heating, because our well water was very hard. The Kansas term for adding lye to the wash water was breaking the water. Everyone told us that we had the best drinking water in Norton County. It was excellent. It was loaded with minerals, but our well water straight from the well would cause the soap to be a scummy mess and ineffective in cleaning the clothes.

Sometimes Mom used homemade soap made from rendered lard, lye, and occasionally she added ashes. This, homemade, soap was formed in to huge ugly wedge shaped bars. It was so harsh that it could eat the hide off a mule; let alone what it did to the clothes. Generally, mom used P & G bar soap, which was much gentler on the clothes. I usually got the job of shaving the soap into very thin shavings so that it would dissolve in the heated water more readily. Mother used to tell me that those who were careless with their money or too lazy to shave a bar of soap bought soap flakes in a box, but never at the Archer's.

Dad's next sequence of accomplishments was to install a pressure water system at the well. What a marvel this was, to just snap on a switch and water would flow through a pipe to the stock tank or into a pail for the house.

As time and my parent's budget allowed, Dad dug a ditch to the house for the water pipe. Plumbing of the house followed. I watched Dad do all of the plumbing in our house. I learned how to cut and thread pipe, install elbows, nipples, and faucets. One of my jobs was to apply joint compound on both male and female threads before the joints, were united and tightened. Not many kids get to have, such, one-on-one instruction in the plumbing trade.

Our house had a large hall clothes closet between two of the bedrooms that dad converted into a bathroom. He installed a flush toilet and the old outhouse was retired. What a luxury this was. No more trips out in the frigid night air of winter to a smelly building that no amount of lime could ever completely clear the air. My folks bought a large cast-iron bathtub that sat upon big cast iron lion's feet. Today that bathtub would bring a handsome price as an antique. Only the cold-water faucet was attached to the water main. Hot water for our baths was still heated on the stove. Filling a ten-gallon wash boiler with a pail from the kitchen sink still meant that some planning had to take place before one could take a bath.

My mechanical education came from watching and learning from my Dad as he continually tackled new challenges. I so clearly remember the days squatting in our attic watching him install the knob and tube insulators that held the electrical wiring. He always took the time to explain what he was doing and how everything worked. He had no formal training or experience in any of these fields, but he could think, ask questions of others, and he was not afraid to tackle any job. How fortunate I was to have such a good teacher.

This little farmstead was far too small to provide a living, but my father was a rural mail carrier and had a salary that supported the family. The farm offered my parents a chance to return to their childhood farm lifestyle. I have strong convictions that both parents wanted my sister and I to have the advantages of both city and farm life. With Dad and Mom taking on the extra work of running a small farm, they had some extra income. This allowed us a few extras that the meager salary from the post office did not provide. Most importantly, it provided them with the link to their childhood environs.

Standing here looking out over the Prairie Dog Creek Valley, I realize how lucky my dad was to have a steady paycheck. Farming was such a big gamble. The timing of planting a crop could be very critical. The chance of getting snow or rain at the right time and in the right amount was a crapshoot. Even when it looked like a good crop was just about to be harvested a hailstorm or a lightning strike in a ripe wheat field not only could wipe out a whole years income, but it often wiped out the farm as well. Payment of mortgage notes to the bank often depended on a whim of Mother Nature.

One hot summer day, Dad and I were on our way to the little town of Lenora. Just about five miles south of Norton, Dad said, "Eldon, see that smoke west of us? That has to be a wheat fire." He turned at the next intersection and drove toward the smoke. It was a wheat fire and the field belonged to one of Dad's mail route patrons. Farmers from everywhere were arriving to help put out the fire. There were two large stacks of wet gunnysacks piled on the ground. Dad and I each grabbed one and we ran to the fire line. Fortunately, there was no strong wind, only a slight breeze blowing from behind us. The farmer who owned the field was already on his tractor plowing the ground up, fifty yards or so ahead of the fire. Lady Luck was with the farmer that day. Only about ten acres burned.

Two lessons I learned that day. One, always keep the wind to your back when fighting a fire and secondly always be prepared when the risk of fire is great. Beating the fire line with wet gunnysacks by many neighbors stopped the fire before it reached the plowed ground. Certainly, it was a loss, but not a disaster.

I STOOD ON A KNOLL SOUTH OF NORTON looking at the place that meant so much to me in my early youth. Before the second summer was over, my father brought home a black and white spotted Shetland pony for my sister and I. We named him Cupid. The addition of the pony increased the livestock inventory on the Archer farm to three. We had two Jersey milk cows that provided us with more milk, and cream than we could use, so there was a surplus that could be sold to the Norton creamery. Our alfalfa field provided enough hay each year to feed two or three milk cows and a small pony.

I STOOD ON A KNOLL SOUTH OF NORTON, on this quiet day in May. Summer vacation for the school kids had just begun. Seeing the kids out of school reminded me of summer vacations on the farm as one exciting adventure after another. Cupid, my Shetland pony, was responsible for many of these adventures. Many mornings Dad would saddle Cupid while he was doing his early morning chores. The pony would be halter-tied to the corral fence when I got up. Dad would already be at the post office sorting the mail for his rural delivery by the time I sat at the kitchen table eating my breakfast. Bridling my pony was easy for me, because he readily took the bit. He loved to be ridden.

Some mornings I would ride alone and other mornings Ann Corder and I would ride our ponies together. Ann was my age and she lived a mile east from our farm. Her Shetland pony was all black and she was a good rider. We rode all over the countryside. Sometimes we rode south into the hills of grass, other times we rode through the timber along the creek bottom. Our ponies loved to run and we gave them every opportunity to gallop to their hearts content. One of our farm neighbors told my Dad one day, "Clyde did you know that Eldon and Ann Corder are running those ponies harder than they should?" "Someone is going to get hurt." Only many years later did Dad tell me of this incident.

One day I was riding alone and Cupid was running flat out. We were on the old milldam road, where the road was cut from the side of a chalk hill that ran parallel to the creek. Suddenly a feral cat jumped out of the grader ditch and ran across the road. It startled Cupid and he stopped on a dime, but I did not. I went sailing over his head and onto the packed hardpan of the road. The wind was knocked out of me, when my chest collided with the road. A momentary Fourth of July fireworks display flashed in my eyes as my head followed my impact. I lay there in the road, pain coursing through my body, and I was gasping for breath. Through bleary eyes that had not yet come into focus, I saw Cupid standing with his head down, reins touching the ground, waiting for me to remount.

When the cobwebs cleared from my brain, and I had regained part of my breath I assessed the damage. I found only a few injuries: a knot on my forehead, a badly bitten lip, and the skin on both elbows were now two bloody spots in the road. They say that a cat has nine lives, but believe me when I say that a boy on a farm has far more than a cat.

I stood on a knoll south of Norton and visions of special friends flashing before me. My sister was nine years older than I was, so with the exception of maybe a game of rummy now and then, naturally we did not play much together. A young energetic boy gets lonely playing by himself every day, so, often on Saturdays during the school year, or any day during school summer vacation, my parents would let me invite one of my special friends out to the farm to play.

We would ride our bikes for miles on the country roads and never meet a car. Playing follow the leader on a bike, can be great fun and generally we made it very challenging. Jumping our bikes over grader ditches or riding and skidding down near vertical dirt banks, occasionally led to some bad spills. Fishing was always popular. We would get the cane poles, dig, a can of worms, and head for the creek. There has never been a boy born who does not thrill to a bouncing cork while a bluegill or a catfish samples the bait.

Our favorite games were playing cowboys and Indians, or cowboy's and. robbers. The game of our imagination usually depended on the last Saturday movie matinee we had seen. Sometimes an argument would occur as to who would be Hop-Along Cassidy, while the other might take on the roll of Roy Rogers. We had a variety of other Heroes to choose from like, The Lone Ranger, Hoot Gibson, The Cisco Kid,

Tom Mix, Zoro, and many others that have faded from my memory. As young boys, we never went any place unless we were armed. Armed with one or two cap pistols, holstered and strapped to our legs, ready for a fast draw. With rolls of paper caps stashed in one of our overall pockets, we could take on the bad-guys anytime. One of our favorite locals for these imaginary gun battles, with the bad-guys, was the soft chalk cliff that paralleled the road down by the milldam. There were vertical crevices starting at the top of the cliff and extending to the road below. Squeezing into one of these crevices, we could take cover during our mock gun battles with the men in the black hats. Narrow ledges offered us the opportunity to side step across the face of the cliff traversing from niche to niche giving us the advantage of the high ground. Many mornings were spent in these make believe games with one of my special friends. Cops and robbers, another popular game, was reserved for times when invited, to their homes in town.

Most of my friends would get to ride Cupid before they went home. Dad knew how important it was for a visiting friend to brag to his parents that he had ridden a horse. I can never remember my dad being too busy to saddle Cupid so that he could add a little something special to their day.

Names, I had not thought of in many years, pushed their way forward from deep recesses in my mind. Bob Madden, Lowell Moody, Roy Hoover, Elmer King, Tom Taylor, Eugene Dobby. Mental images of their faces matched their names as I recalled the good times. Suddenly, dark, murky clouds of sadness interrupted my reverie.

The fun and games were gone as I recalled one morning during my summer vacation. I was eating breakfast and it was at a time Dad should be starting out on his mail route. Instead, he had just driven into our driveway. This was extremely unusual. The U. S. Postal Department had very strict rules, and Dad was a person committed to following the rules.

Mother told me to finish my breakfast and she left the kitchen and walked out to meet him. I watched as they stood by the windmill for a long time talking. I could not read the somber expression on their faces as they headed for the house.

Upon entering the kitchen, Dad said, "son I have some really bad news to tell you. Your friend Eugene Dobby is dead. Sometime during the night, His dad took a .22 rifle and shot every member of the family in the head and then he killed himself." I was probably ten or eleven years old. Death was new to me. Adults do not discuss death with a child my age unless it is required. I have re-lived this terrible morning many times during my life. Etched in my brain as if it were stone, I remember my reactions. Why did Eugene's dad kill every member of his family? I struggled with the thought that I would never see Eugene again. The finality of this event hit me extremely hard. Eugene would never be coming to the farm, nor would he and I roller skate together or play marbles during school recess.

My mind just locked up, I did not cry but I knew that I had to be by myself. I just could not understand what had happened. I knew that Eugene had two brothers and a sister. Why, did this terrible thing happen? Without a word, I went out to the side yard where we split wood on a huge upturned cross-section of a cotton wood log. Under the shade of a big Box Elder tree, I sat down on this big weathered chopping block.

I have no idea how long I sat there. It may have been a few minutes, it may have been an hour, I, have no idea. I kept playing over in my mind the good times we had had together, since kindergarten. His round cherub face with his short round pug nose played before me as if he were here in front of me. Again the question of "why, why" kept tormenting me.

There was no lump in my throat, tears in my eyes, only emptiness in my stomach. Today, I honestly think that God may have helped me cope with this, the worst event to happen in my young life. Sitting there alone with grief paralyzing my mind, no answers came to me then, nor has any to this very day. I am certain, however, that some very strong and vicious demons had tormented the mind of Eugene's dad.

I stood on a knoll South of Norton; remembering how special fall was to me. Cooler days and chilly nights marked the beginning of fall. Jack Frost, the mythical artist, first painted the leaves of the Sumac plants in vermilion and various shades of reds that deepened in color as fall developed. Within a few days, Mr. Frost would turn his attention to less tender plants and trees. For these, his choice of colors was bright and subtle shades of yellow and many hues of gold. He used care in balancing his color-spectrum with tans and browns. I remember walking home from school, with the acrid smell of burning leaves permeating the air. For me, the pungent smell of burning leaves and Halloween go together.

Fall marked the beginning of new activities on the Archer farm. It was time to take down the coal oil cook stove used in the kitchen during the hot months of summer. The oil stove was replaced with the heavy cast iron wood-burning cook stove. It is strange that my fondest memory of that stove is the oven that toasted slices of my mother's homemade bread to such a beautiful golden hue.

Fall was a time for new smells. I remember the great aroma of home cured ham frying in the big iron skillet as my Mother prepared breakfast. Branded in my memory, were the smoky taste of the ham and the texture of the thick rind. Many weeks before my mother had hand-rubbed the ham with liquid smoke, curing salt, and sugar. This helped to preserve the meat and gave it that exquisite flavor.

It was a busy time. Late vegetables and fruit had to be canned. There were potatoes to be dug, cleaned, and stored, in the cellar for us to use all winter. It was also a time for butchering. There were Cabbages from our garden, waiting to be picked, sliced, salted, and placed in stone jars, for nature to pickle into sour kraut.

To feed the big iron cook stove, wood needed to be cut, split, and then stacked, in a neat rick. That first fall Dad cut the logs by hand with a crosscut saw that today hangs in my workshop. The following season he bought a big circular saw blade that was three feet in diameter. He fastened this huge blade to one end of a car axle and attached a wide belt pulley on the other end. He then attached this unit to a steel frame with a bearing assembly. He made a sliding wooden table and fastened it to the steel frame. The table held the logs in position as Dad pushed the table forward, the saw sliced through the log. These mechanical, labor saving devices were known as buzz saws.

An old Ford model T car engine supplied the power to the ten-foot long four-inch wide belt that powered the saw. On a quiet day, the saw's piercing scream, was heard for well over a mile. Our neighbors, up and down the Prairie Dog, knew when Dad was sawing logs, into stove-lengths. Later, they were split into firewood. One of my after school chores was to split a pile of wood and stack it on the wood rack. Fall, is the summary of summer, and the prelude to winter, and a provider of many wonderful memories.

I stood on a knoll south of Norton and in my mind, I watched fall release its grip on time. Nickel sized snowflakes individually crocheted by the angels of winter floated quietly to the ground. Soon a blanket of soft white snow would embrace the land. It was sled time. Dad would pull my sister and I on our *Red Bud* sled behind the *Model-A Ford* roadster. We would go breezing down the road with loose snow flying in our faces whipped up by the roadster's spinning wheels. It was a time for spills, thrills, laughter and yelps.

Red cheeks, cold tingling toes, and numbed fingers were warmed in front of the open oven of our big cook stove. I can smell the stench and see the steam rising from wet cotton jersey gloves drying on the open oven door. Under the stove were wet shoes, drying in the radiant heat of the stove. Sprawled behind the stove, *Bob*, our Fox Terrier dog was snoozing. He was tired from his running and yelping behind two kids on a sled. Now warm and dry, he was sound asleep in his favorite spot. On top of the stove, Mom often stirred cream-rich oyster stew, yellowed by a dollop of home churned butter. A big bowl of oyster stew augmented by a couple of slices of fresh homemade bread would be our supper. What a great way to warm our innards on a cold winter's night. Dessert might be hot apple pie, kept waiting for us in the warming oven at the top of the stove.

I STOOD ON A KNOLL SOUTH OF NORTON

    Winters in Northwest Kansas can be bitterly cold. I remember many winter nights when the mercury in the thermometer was nudging zero, and my Dad and I would take a walk down the road a half-mile or more. I remember how still and cold it would be. The air was so cold and dense that it seemed as if it could crack like sub-zero ice on a lake. The only sound was the squeak of ultra-dry snow crunching under the soles our boots as we walked in the winter silence.

    Imbedded in my memory of these special times is the brilliance of the silver sky, illuminated by the billions of stars. Their soft light illuminated the snow allowing our vision to penetrate the night. The air was so pure and clear and the starlight so bright. I so clearly remember the magical, peaceful spell embracing this land of quiet beauty. Such mystical splendor cannot be adequately described. It can only be experienced. When Dad and I would return, often as not, the aroma of fresh hot buttered popcorn greeted us as we entered the kitchen. Mother would have a big dishpan of popcorn waiting for our return. Today in the busy world we live in, one popular religious sect has set aside one night a week for family time. Growing up in my family, every night was family time.

    I realize that this was a different time and a different set of circumstances. When the sun went down and the supper dishes were done, it was time for all kinds of games or listening to the radio. My folks owned an *Atwater Kent* radio, which at the time was the best that money could buy. The radio was incased in a big steel box twice the size of today's VCR. Inside there were many vacuum tubes that were as large as a 150-watt light bulb. Each tube had its function in capturing the radio waves from the very few radio stations that were available. WIBW at Topeka, Kansas was our nearest station, and most reliable for reception. On the front of the radio were four big dials. I never knew what each dial did, because Dad or Mom always tuned it in. The speaker was a big horn like affair exactly as the one pictured in the *Buster Brown* shoe logo.

Our favorite program was Amos and Andy. The program came on every evening at 6:00. The same program was repeated at 9:00. Occasional I was allowed to stay up after my bedtime, if we missed the early evening program. Two very talented white performers furnished the voices for a variety of black characters in the program. My favorite character was Lightning. The mental image of this character was that, of a very skinny, not too bright Negro man. His slow protracted speech depicted someone moving at the speed of cold molasses being poured from a mason jar. Cold weather and good radio reception go together. I have such great memories of those winter evenings. It was not only the radio programs, but it was games of *Rook*, rummy, checkers, and caroms that filled our evenings and made life so full.

I STOOD ON A KNOLL SOUTH OF NORTON with vignettes of Christmases past. Each pleasure of my memory was vying for my attention. I remember a young boy's desire to unwrap a box on Christmas Eve to find an electric train, only to find a zephyr that wound with a key. Lessons of anticipation, pleasures, and some disappointments were all part of growing up.

Once just before Christmas a raging blizzard had kept my sister and I at home. Boredom and my curiosity got the better of me and I begged my mother to let me open just one present before Christmas. There was a small gift-wrapped box tied to one of the tinsel decorated boughs of our Christmas tree. I was certain that it contained a gyroscope top. This was a toy, I desperately wanted; yet, it would not spoil my Christmas Eve fun if I opened it now. In my mother's wisdom and to satisfy my begging, she agreed to let me open this one present. To my surprise, my sister had placed one of her tiny china dolls in the box as a joke. Why do I remember this tiny piece of film, perhaps it was a lesson learned. A deal is a deal.

One of my greatest Christmas gifts was a new pair of high top lace leather boots. They were the deluxe model with solid leather heals and a jackknife pouch stitched thigh high. In the pouch was a jackknife, with many blades and useful tools. Another box contained a new set of nickel-plated ice skates. The new boots and skates meant improved pleasure of ice-skating on the creek. No longer would I struggle with leather strap skates and oxford shoes that offered no ankle support. Now I could play shinny with the best of my friends from town.

All of my friends lived in town and many days of our Christmas vacation were spent skating on the creek. Every year we looked forward to a time when the ice on the creek would be thick enough to support our weight. Almost every winter someone would test the ice too soon, and an ice water soaking would result. I was probably the guiltiest, of the group. Most generally we would only go in up over our knees, so we would build a bon fire to dry out. We could usually find a log to sit on around the fire waiting for our socks and pant legs to dry out. To speed the drying of our socks we would find a couple of sticks to insert into them and hold them over the heat of the fire until they were semi-dry. A kid quickly learns the difference between wool and cotton socks and how much quicker wool dries out. There is also a decidedly different smell between scorched wool and scorched cotton.

Hockey was only a word in the dictionary to kids from Norton. Shinny was our game. A good shinny stick was either a one-inch thick root or a limb from a tree about three feet long with a sixty to ninety degree bend at one end. We would break our shinny sticks to size leaving about four inches beyond the bend; this became the lethal part of the stick. A good stick had a striking end heavier than the shaft. I use the word striking, because our games had no finesse. Our puck was usually an empty six-ounce Carnation condensed milk can. We used our shinny stick as an angry Irishman might use a shillelagh. The difference was that we were quickly converting the milk can in to a crumpled mass of crunched metal.

The goals at each end of our creek arena were stones collected from the creek bank and placed about four feet apart. We never used a goalie. First, we did not know that they used goalies in real games of hockey, and secondly, no one would be dumb enough to face a crumpled metal projectile struck with all the power we could muster by a full swing of our shinny stick. There were very few rules of the game. It was mostly a game of speed and mayhem. Equipment requirements were a pair of ice-skates and for a few lucky kids a pair of leather gloves or mittens. Everyone who played shinny, eventually, would acquire one or more permanent scars. What a rough and tumble game it was. It is a wonder someone did not get seriously hurt, but oh, what fun we had.

I STOOD ON A KNOLL SOUTH OF NORTON remembering the first Christmas Eve at the farm. The supper dishes were washed and stored in the pantry and Dad said that he had a surprise Christmas present for Hazel and me. He said that is was a gift from one of his patrons on his mail route. Of course, Hazel and I were eager to find out what it was. Dad said that he would go out in the garage and bring it in to us. He returned with a large cardboard box that contained a fox terrier puppy. This was the first pet my sister and I had ever owned.

The puppy was just as excited, as my sister and I were. We named this little white bundle of energy Bob. Little did any of us realize at that moment in time, what a great gift our family had received. For the next fifteen years, this dog provided our family with wonderful experiences and pleasures. True to his breed, he was a hunter. Before he was a year old, he was treeing opossums, raccoons, and stray cats.

My father always claimed that he could tell by the excitement and pitch of Bob's bark whether he had a wild animal treed or just a stray cat. It was always at night that this treeing took place. If the pitch of Bob's bark were just right, Dad would get up, dress, get his big five-cell flashlight, strap on his revolver, and head toward the fracas. Each year Dad kept a tally of the raccoons, skunks opossums, and even an occasional badger that Bob would corner.

One very early morning, long before the sun had even given a thought to rising over the eastern horizon, I awoke to the all most uncontrolled laughter of my parents. My mind was still muddled with sleep, but such raucous laughter was highly unusual. I had to get out of bed and investigate. The photograph embed in my mind today is as clear in detail at it was at that time.

My folks were in the kitchen, and they were a mess. My dad's overalls were wet to his waist, but you should have seen my mother. She was in her nightgown, totally wet and covered by mud. When they saw me, standing in the door, they realized what a sight this must present. It was beyond their ability to control their laughter. As soon as one started to tell me what happened, the other would break out in laughter; and then they would interrupt one another as they tried to tell me what happened. Finally, with tears rolling down their cheeks, I got the whole story.

Sometime during the night, Dad heard Bob screaming in his highest most excited bark. Dad dressed, and started toward the creek just below our chicken house. Bob was on the other side of the creek looking up and running around a big cottonwood tree, barking furiously. It was mid summer and the foliage was so dense, that Dad's five cell flash light could not pick up the reflective glow of an animals eyes in the tree.

While my Dad was continuing to search the tree, Bob began to swim back across the creek. Latter Dad said, "That dog had never fooled me before, but I couldn't figure why he was coming back across the creek and leaving his prey. Bob reached the bank and clawed his way up onto dry ground. He ran to another big cottonwood tree and started circling it and barking as before. "I thought the dog had lost his mind." Dad went on to tell the story. He finally decided that there was a raccoon in each of the trees.

The strong beam of the flashlight finally reflected the green glow of a raccoon's eyes high up in the tree next to Dad. Once he had the beam of the flashlight centered on the critter, he dispatched the animal with a single shot from the 22 Caliber Harrington Richardson revolver that now hangs in its' holster in my closet in Phoenix. Dad was an expert shot with that revolver. At fifty feet, I have seen him place five shots in the bull's-eye of a paper target. You could cover the holes with a penny.

As soon as the animal hit the ground, Bob started swimming back to the far side of the creek with Dad wading, hip deep, behind him. In the middle of the creek, Dad slipped on a rock and dropped his big flashlight. It continued to glow underwater, so he easily retrieved it. Crawling up the muddy, slippery bank on the far side was no small chore but eventually he was standing at the base of the big cottonwood. This time it was easier to pick up the reflected light in the eyes of the raccoon, as he was now moving out on a limb. He was looking for a way to jump to the next tree and try for an escape. The light from the flashlight began to fade and finally it went out. The water had seeped into the flashlight and shorted in out. Dad was afraid to leave and go back to the house for another flashlight, for fear the raccoon would escape, so he began shouting, in hopes of waking Mother. When Mom heard Dad's shout, she rushed out of the house in her nightgown, thinking that he might be hurt.

She followed his shouts until they could communicate with one another. She returned to the house and got another light. She walked down the hill behind our chicken house to the creek bank.

She walked out to the edge of bank so that she could hand the light to Dad once he waded back across the creek. Mother was shinning the beam of her flashlight on the water just ahead of Dad as he waded toward her. Accidents are most generally moments of utter stupidity. This was one of those moments. The bank was about three feet above the water level. It had been undercut, by beavers and the current of the creek.

Her situation of being the loyal, helpful, wife, guiding her husband by her torch beam, suddenly changed dramatically. She had stepped out too far on the bank. Whoosh, the bank caved in taking a large chunk of earth and my mom into the water. My mother was short, and she was quite heavy. The combination of the large chunk of earth and the size of my Mother must have developed a tidal wave in the creek, the likes of which it had never experienced. At this point of the story, I began to laugh, as my imagination began playing the scene as if I had been there. I could see her wallowing in the mud and water, holding the flashlight up high so that it too would not be flooded.

The score: Two raccoons, that would never steal eggs from our chicken house again, a very proud fox terrier dog, two wet, muddy, but very happy parents; and a son who was lucky enough to have shared this experience.

As I stood here on this knoll with tears of joy blurring my vision another memory screamed for attention, as if Bob wanted me to remember a very emotional episode in his colorful and eventful life. This great piece of memory was as clear as a flawless diamond refracting mental images flashing at the speed of light, all vying for my time of contemplation. This memory of the past was branded in the recess of my mind as deeply and clearly as a glowing hot iron leaves a lifetime mark to the flank of a calf at branding time. There are stories upon stories, experiences upon experiences, but none are more emotional than when suddenly one of our family members disappeared.

One morning Dad finished the morning chores and came to the house for breakfast. He announced that Bob, our Fox Terrier dog was missing. This was totally unusual because every morning Bob waited at the door to go with Dad to the barn for the morning milking of our two Jersey cows. My Dad and that dog were inseparable. We were all very concerned. Bob once had gotten in a fight with a badger out in the road in front of our house and that fight ended in a draw. The loud noise of the violence awakened Dad from a sound sleep. He quickly dressed, grabbed his big flashlight and revolver and tore out the kitchen door. Arriving where the terrible ruckus had occurred, Bob was lying on one side of the road smeared in blood and panting for breath. The badger equally in bad shape was doing likewise on the other side of the road. Dad umpired the fight bringing it to a close with a .22 bullet through the head of the badger. We talked about this episode and were worried that something like this might have occurred again. Bob might be severely injured or maybe even dead.

Dad had to go to work and my sister and I had to go to school so we could only hope that Bob would show up. When Hazel and I came home from school, Bob had not returned. We talked about the possibility that a car could have hit him but Dad explained that he had driven all of the roads within three to four miles of our farm and no dog.

After the evening chores were done and we had eaten our dinner, Dad said, "I am going to saddle Dan and ride up along the Prairie Dog Creek where I know Bob often hunts and see if I can find him." I begged to go along on my pony Cupid but he said, "not this time son; tomorrow is a school day and I may be gone until the early hours of the morning." I had reached an age where I thought I was too old to cry, but oh how I wanted to. Not because I couldn't go but because my dog was gone and we didn't know what had happened to him. I went outside and gathered up "Tiny", our Rat Terrier dog and brought her into the kitchen where she lay on my lap as I sat on the floor by our wood cook stove. It was early Fall and there was a nip in the air. The warmth of the stove and the love from Tiny got me through the evening until it was time to go to bed.

Whenever my Dad and I were separated I always worried that something would happen to him. This worry plagued me as far back as my memory allows and on this particular night it was almost more than I could stand. A hole in one's heart from worry is impossible to describe. I envisioned all kinds of things that could happen to Dad riding through the woods with only his five-celled flashlight and the night vision of Dan to lead their way. At some point this gnawing aching turmoil subsided as I fell into a restless sleep.

I woke with a start as I heard my bedroom door open and my mother said, "Eldon, wake up, Dad is back". I ran to the kitchen and there he was sitting in our big wooden rocking chair by the fire holding Bob all wrapped up in a big fluffy bath towel. Was I too old to cry, not by a long shot! I begin sobbing and laughing at the same time, with tears of joy pouring down my cheeks. My dog was alive and my Dad was safely home!

Dad sat rocking in the chair stroking Bob's head with tender love as he lay in his lap softly whimpering. I didn't know why but I was soon to find out. Dad explained that Bob was dehydrated and he was rationing his water in small amounts at a time to save him from stomach cramps.

Dad began to tell us about his trip up along the Prairie Dog. Our little farm had about four acres of woods along the Creek. He and Dan covered every foot searching every hole in and around the roots of the giant Cottonwood trees that grew so close together, they're wide spread canopies nearly touched. Just enough sunlight filtered through their canopies to allow a ground cover of grass and wild flowers. It was an idyllic place for rabbits, squirrels, and a variety of wild life. It took Dad an hour or so to thoroughly scour this wooded area. He found no trace of our dog or any evidence that anything was amiss so he opened the gate in our fence and moved on up the creek on to Elmer Fisher's property.

He continued to call Bob's name and continued to cast the beam of that powerful flashlight in every direction that he thought might offer a clue to his search. He had ridden well over a mile and was within a quarter of a mile of Elmer Fisher's farmhouse, when he thought he heard a slight noise. He wasn't sure that his ears and his imagination were playing tricks with his mind but he sat very quietly on Dan listening intently. Then he heard it again. This time he knew it was coming from the base of a big Oak tree that was anchored into the ground at the bottom of a small hill.

By this time the beam of the flashlight now was very dim. The batteries had been working overtime. Spurring Dan toward the tree he called Bob's name but still he could not see anything. Then when he was within a few feet of the tree he heard a little whine and he saw the rump of a small white dog with a bobbed tail wagging furiously. It was Bob! He leaped off of Dan and in one giant stride he was beside his precious friend. In all of my life I never saw my Dad cry but in my heart I know he did that night.

Dad continued his story telling us that Bob was trapped with a wire noose around his neck. This type of snare trap slides easily over an animal's head but has enough tension not to allow the head to be pulled back out. An animal as small as a squirrel could go right through such a noose but larger animals would be live trapped. Bob had barked for so many hours that he was totally without voice. He could barely whimper and he had been trapped so long that he probably would not have lasted through the night. The noose had been cleverly placed around a big hole at the base of the tree. Many years of rot had hollowed out the center of this century old Oak up ten feet or more. At the top of the cavity was a hole through the tree where a limb was once attached. Probably a windstorm had broken off the limb exposing a perfect escape hole. Dad reasoned that Bob had chased a squirrel into the ground level hole and tried to follow it. The squirrel went up inside the hollow tree out of the escape hole and it scampered on up the tree leaving Bob with the wire noose around his neck.

I had seen such traps pictured in my Boy Scout Manual so I knew what Dad was describing. In one of the leather saddle bags attached behind Dad's saddle was a pair of fence-mending pliers. Several quick snips and the spring steel noose was no longer a trap for dog or wild animal. The short pieces of wire left on the ground would let the trapper know someone had been very upset in finding the snare.

My mother was really angry. She immediately accused Elmer Fisher of setting the trap but Dad was not so sure. He said that it could have been Charles Dawley, a boy a few years older than I was who lived a mile south of our farm. Dad pointed out that setting the trap was perfectly legal. Trapping licenses had not even been thought of. In fact I doubt at that time there were any fish and game laws in effect in Kansas. We were in the heart of the depression and the loss of a few chickens to a hungry Raccoon was a major loss to anyone. Mom agreed with Dad that the important thing was the trap no longer existed and we had our dog back. Occasionally Bob would lick Dad's face and the movement of the towel by the wagging of his stubby little tail, told us everything would turn out all right.

❧

I stood on a knoll south of Norton remembering that it was not always good times during the 30's. There were the dark brown, tending toward black clouds of dust swirling thousands of feet in the air. These forbidding monsters would roll in from the south or the north and turn day into night. Going to school in clear early morning sunlight, carrying our lunch and a dust mask was no guarantee that it would be a fine day. By noon, the dust in the classroom could be so thick that it would be necessary to turn on the lights. The dirty red halo surrounding the ceiling lights meant that it was time for the Principal to call our parents and have them come and take us home. No one was allowed to leave, lest we be lost in the dust storm that raged outside.

Farm crops, were blown loose from the ground or they were covered by inches of loose soil. Fences disappeared under drifts of dirt that left only a couple of inches of fence pots reminding one of field territories, now no longer important. People, too dumb, or too poor became survivors. The other's, gathered what few belongings they could and fled to California.

❧

I STOOD ON A KNOLL SOUTH OF NORTON and I realize that today these are nightmare movies, but to me as a youth, it was just a happening, that was to be taken in stride. My Parents never complained. They just made the best of any situation. This shaped my life more than I had any knowledge of as a child. Looking back on the dark days of the dust storms, the extremely poor people affected by the great depression and the two years of grasshopper invasion were viewed by my young mind very differently than seen by my parents.

My only recollection of any sense of defeat from either of my parents was my mother's reaction one spring morning. Early in the spring, Dad and Mom had converted our front yard to a large vegetable garden. As soon as the ice melted from the Prairie Dog, Dad installed an irrigation pump on the creek bank to pump water up the hill and in to little irrigation ditches to water the plants. It was the finest garden my parents had ever grown. Mother was so proud of the vegetables it produced.

One day there was a brown cloud in the southern sky and we thought that it was another dust storm approaching? Not so, it was an invasion of grasshoppers. Next morning our garden was gone, eaten to the ground. Even the leaves of our Chinese elm trees, were being stripped by this savage hoard of insects. The ground was alive with this crawling grasshopper scourge. I had never seen my mother cry until that awful day.

The grasshopper scourge lasted for two years. I have the feeling that when I tell people about this terrible grasshopper plague, they think that I am a teller of tall tales, but not so. I cannot even come close to explaining how bad it really was. I know that with the insect controls we have today, it is hard to believe that the black top highways became slick with the crushed bodies of these flying, jumping, and creeping insects.

One job I hated the most was when dad would assign to me the job of washing off the grasshopper mess on the front of our family car. With box of Arm & Hammer soda, a bucket of water and a sponge I would attempt to wash off the yellow and green smears on the front of our V-8 Ford. Attempt was all you could do, because the body fluids of smashed grasshoppers, adhered to the paint like hardened glue. When we would drive to McCook, Nebraska to shop, Dad would have stop and clean the windshield two or three times on both legs of the trip from grasshopper snear.

Grasshoppers have a voracious appetite and they ate the farm crops as soon as they came up in the spring. The Norton Farm Bureau developed poison wheat bran flakes to be sprinkled on the ground in an attempt to control them. Grasshoppers will eat anything; unfortunately, the poison laded bran would also have killed our chickens so we had to search for other methods of control.

My Dad's ingenuity came to the forefront again. He went to the tin shop in Norton and had metal pans made. These pans were four feet long, two feet wide and four inches deep. He placed them on a buck rake that was attached in front of our *Model A Ford*. Behind the metal pans, he installed a vertical sheet of metal. Used motor oil was easy to obtain at no cost at the service stations. They were glad to get rid of it. This thick, black, dirty, oil was poured into the pans to a depth of a couple of inches.

Dad would drive this contraption over our alfalfa field when the alfalfa was short enough not be damaged by the tires of the car. The grasshoppers would jump up in front of the rake, fly into the vertical sheet of metal, and drop into the used motor oil. When the oil became so thick with grasshoppers that new ones were not immersed enough, allowing some to escape, Dad would drive to the grader ditch between the field and the side of the road, dump the oil soaked insets and light them afire. Time after time, Dad replenished the oil and by continuing to drive over the alfalfa field, eventually the majority of the grasshoppers were eliminated, at least for that moment in time. It certainly was not a perfect solution, but it worked.

Usually the alfalfa would grow fast enough that we could get a cutting before a new infestation of grasshoppers could start stripping the leaves severely. Once we had the crop cut, and safely put in the haymow, it was time to repeat the eradication program. I know that most people find it hard to believe a tale like this but I could write a small book about this terrible scourge. It was not just the crops they ate, but the voracious devils even ate holes in the dinning room curtains. Mother had to keep a sharp eye out for any that might get in to the house. The many years of drought, the depression, the dust bowl days and the grasshopper scourge have been well documented, as a part of Western Kansas' history.

I STOOD ON A KNOLL SOUTH OF NORTON, with the pages of my memory diary flipping by, like dry leaves blowing in an autumn breeze. One of those memory pages stopped in clear focus. It was the day I soloed in our *Model-A Ford* roadster. I was helping Dad mow our alfalfa field West of the barn. There was no money in my parent's budget for a tractor, so they made the best of what they had. We used the Ford as a tractor to pull all of our farm equipment.

I STOOD ON A KNOLL SOUTH OF NORTON

Our mowing machine was designed to be pulled by a team of horses. We had no horses, but we had the Ford. Dad shortened the tongue of the mower and installed a trailer hitch on the *Model A*. As soon as I was old enough, I rode the mowing machine while Dad drove the car. At the end of each swath, it was my job to lift the cutting bar, as the rig was being turned to start a new swath. My weight, alone, was not enough to overcome the inertia necessary to lift the bar. I had to make a little hop and come down hard on to the iron foot lever. If I hopped high, enough my downward momentum was just enough to overcome the weight of the cutting bar.

Dad was a great coach. He always made me feel like a team member when we worked together. After the field was cut, and the hay had time to dry, He would attach a short tongued, hay rake to the back of the roadster. My job was to ride the rake. When the rake had accumulated enough hay in the rake, I would step on a steel pedal and dump the hay.

After the first dump, it was my job to dump each rake full of hay at the same spot leaving windrows of coiled hay. It was tricky to lean just the right time to step on the pedal. The rake was easy to dump because the forward motion of the rake tripped the hay-loaded tines, leaving a nicely rounded coil of hay. Dressed in my faded bib overalls I was proud of doing a good job. I soon learned to anticipate when to step on the pedal, so that the rows of hay would lie in a straight line. A pat on the back, or a good word from my Dad built my pride; so important to a young kid.

I so clearly remember a particular day. We had completed raking the hay and my Dad called me over to the car. He pointed out some loose hay lying on the ground that we had missed or it had slipped between the tines of the rake. He said that he wanted me to drive the rig between the windrows of hay and rake up the loose hay. When the rake was full, I was to drive over where he would be working and he would dump lit. The intensity of excitement that shot through me at that moment maybe has never been repeated. My Dad was going to trust me to take on this very important job, alone.

I already knew how to shift the gears. He had taught me how to back the car up, so he could attach the various pieces of machinery that we had. Backing up a foot or so or going ahead short distances was one thing, but driving around six acres of a hay field all by myself was something else. My Dad was entrusting to me, a seven year old, with this responsibility all by myself!

I was so small that to see out of the windshield I had to sit on my feet. Once I shifted the car into the gear I wanted, I would tuck my legs and feet up under me. I used the hand throttle, attached to the steering column, to regulate the speed. What a day it was, I did as my Dad had instructed, and when the rake was full of hay, I drove over where he was working. I moved the hand throttle up to slow, slipped my legs from under me and planted my feet on the clutch and brake pedals.

I knew how important it was to disengage the clutch before applying the brake, or I would kill the engine. If I killed the engine, it would have told Dad that I had failed in the instructions he had given to me. Once he was seated on the rake, I engaged the gears, increased my speed with the throttle, and moved forward. The cogs in the right wheel engage in the iron hub and the forward motion lifted the rake and dumped the roll of hay. Once the hay rake was dumped, I would stop, so that Dad could dismount. He would continue bunching the hay into small stacks that later would be loaded on to the hayrack.

Not everything went perfect, however. There was a slight dent put into my ego that afternoon. I had my first car wreck. Nothing serious, just a headlight bent from forward to vertical. On the last pass when I picked up Dad, he motioned me to a corner at the far end of the field to pick up some loose hay. He was going to ride until we completed the task. We gathered the hay and I headed toward the hayrack to dump it and save extra work bunching it.

I was so busy with all of my mechanical duties and I was looking back to watch my dad when I drove the right front fender in under the corner of the hayrack. The right front headlight was bent straight up. My heart was in my mouth and I was on the verge of tears when my Dad laughed and said, "hey, son, you did a good job today." "Don't worry about the light, it's easy to bend back." Just remember how easily accidents can happen." That evening at dinner, Dad told my Mother what a good a job I had done. There was no mention of the light. My Dad and I were great pals.

A diary helps us to summarize the day just spent, and in the future, a reminder of important events that we might have forgotten. Standing here on this knoll today was just the reverse. My memory provided me with a day's diary entry of my youth.

I STOOD ON A KNOLL SOUTH OF NORTON, reflecting on flashes of loneliness, or were they moments of complete tranquility. I am not sure. It was hard to sort out. In my mind, there were certain sounds associated with these experiences of growing up on a farm. From sunrise to sunset on a farm or ranch there is too much to do for one to get lonely. It is that quiet time after the sun has dropped below the horizon and twilight lingers, waiting for the darkness of night to descend. Then certain sounds lingering in my memory, triggered a sense of loneliness. I remember those evenings when the total stillness was violated by the whump, whump, whump, of the huge one cylinder diesel engine of Norton's light plant. We lived far enough away from the plant that only on very quiet evenings, could we hear the deep, rhythmic throb of the diesel engine providing the power to supply Norton with electricity. Maybe it wasn't the sound so much as the never-ending throbbing beat like the tic tock of a pendulum clock.

Sometimes during a quiet summer night, we might faintly hear a John Deere tractor far off in the distance. We often referred to the John Deer tractor as a one-lunger. Its single cylinder engine had a distinctive high-pitched popping sound. It was like no other sound in the world, but today, it has long been silenced, by modern technology. A higher pitch and shorter rhythm did not have quite the affect on me, as did the big bass rumble of the power plant.

Loneliness cannot be described it can only be experienced. It is an emotion without an on switch. It is just happens. Sometimes the hoot of an owl high in a cottonwood tree down by the creek, calling to its mate, would trigger a pang of loneliness in me, but certainly not in the owl. It was just the beginning of their night's work to find field mice to feed to a pair of owlets waiting in a hollow of a tree. The chirping of crickets, or the yip, yip, yodeling of a family of coyotes; always triggered my emotions.

Nearly any summer evening we could sit out on the porch and hear a serenade of coyotes, far off in the grass hills south of our farm. My father would tell me that we were hearing the ghosts of Plains Indians who once roamed through Kansas in search of Buffalo. He would tell me, that, the long mournful howl of a lone male coyote, was the voice of a warrior who had fallen in battle. Then he would squeeze my knee, and give me a big smile just to let me know that it was all right to pretend.

Savoring these tiny moments of loneliness or interludes of tranquility, whatever they were, make me appreciate how lucky to have experienced them.

I STOOD ON A KNOLL SOUTH OF NORTON and I realized what an important part that *Ford Model-A* roadster had played in my life. I remember the day that Mom drove Dad, my sister, and I to Phillipsburg to take delivery of that car. This new 1930 shiny black roadster was the most exciting car I had ever seen. The dealer had folded back the black cloth top, making it seem even smaller that it was. It was serviced and ready for us to drive it back to Norton. As I recall it was late summer, and on the way home we ran into a very light shower of rain, but it was enough that we stopped and put up the top.

Within a few days, Dad had wooden frames fashioned from oak with sliding glass windows. The window frames were bolted, to the top of the doors. These sliding glass windows replaced the cloth side curtains. This was to be his mail delivery car and side curtains would not keep out snow and cold winds of Northwestern Kansas's winter blizzards. When Dad pulled up beside a mailbox he could easily slide-open the glass and put the mail in the box. These sliding glass windows were just one of his many innovations that I remember. By being my Dad's shadow, I was learning to think about ways to improve things or find solutions to a problem.

I rode with my Dad on his mail route, every opportunity that I got. I have ridden thousands of miles in that Ford in all kinds of weather. My clearest memories are of trips when the weather was bad. Dad's route had 6 miles of blacktop, 24 miles of, usually well graded graveled road, and 32 miles of dirt road, rarely graded. In the winter, Dad carried a big scoop shovel in the turtle so he could open up snowdrifts that had closed the road. When I had the opportunity to go, there was a smaller shovel for me. My dad was totally dedicated to the Rural Mail Carrier's Motto; "The Mail Must go Through". If he could not get through on the roads, he would take off through pastures and fields to get the mail delivered.

There were occasions, after a big snowstorm, that it would be impossible to get through to some of his patrons. In many of the situations he would call the snowbound patron from a neighbor's house and ask them if they would like him leave their mail at their neighbor's.

The snowbound family could saddle up a horse and ride over to their neighbors to get their mail. Having grown up on a farm, my Dad knew how lonesome it gets when you are snowbound. Any mail, and especially if there was a catalogue, commonly referred to as a wish book, could take the edge off that loneliness. Dad's patrons have whiled away hundreds of hours thumbing through the latest issues of Sears Roebuck, Montgomery Ward, and Spiegel catalogues. When new issues arrived the old issues were transported to the outhouse for recycling to another purpose.

Whatever it took, Dad's dedication to getting the mail delivered was paramount. I remember one winter's day when Dad and I scooped the better part of a mile of road to get the mail delivered. I never questioned his dedication, but boy was I tired. The top of both of my big toes had become frost bitten. When we finished the job and were back in the car, I took off my boots to warm my feet in the warm air of the heater. The tops of my toes were chalk white. For years, afterward the top of my toes would itch unmerciful whenever they became too warm. I loved trying to match my dad shovel by shovel that day, but I sure could have done without the frostbite.

I STOOD ON A KNOLL SOUTH OF NORTON, the cool breeze of May caressing my cheeks and bringing the scent of blooming alfalfa, ripe and ready for mowing. When spring was in its prime; it was time to go fishing. Our whole family loved to fish but no one enjoyed it more than my Grandmother Nicholas. After my grandfather died, she came to visit us from time to time. She loved to come in the spring because she loved to fish. There was a long deep hole in the Prairie Dog creek just about a hundred yards from our house. Nearly always, we could catch some nice size catfish from this favorite spot.

We would spade up a can of fish worms from the garden, gather up the cane poles and head for the creek. I feel sorry for people who have never had the thrill of watching a cork bobbing up and down on the water when a fish starts messing with the bait. The action usually starts with tiny concentric rings radiating and expanding outward from the cork. Then the rings become more pronounced and the excitement builds. It is a lesson in patience. As the fish samples the bait, it is hard to wait for the cork to go clear under and stay for a few seconds before setting the hook. Setting the hook too soon is a missed opportunity.

    When my Grandmother's cork would go under she would get so excited, she would rear back lifting the pole, line, and fish straight up and into a full arc. For a brief moment, it became a flying fish. It was my job to remove the fish from the hook and put them on the stringer. It was easy to remove the fish that Grandma Nicholas caught, because they were stunned when they hit the ground after their aerial flight. I can hear her, now in my mind's eye with that hearty belly laugh every time she caught a fish. I hope heaven has a catfish hole. If it does, there you will find my Grandmother Nicholas.

I STOOD ON A KNOLL SOUTH OF NORTON, looking back over nearly seventy years of memory. I was looking at a time when a bicycle was a boy's most prized possession. It provided the freedom of quick transportation that putting one foot in front of the other did not. My first bike was a used twenty-inch model that my dad brought home one sunny spring day. I was just big enough to reach the pedals, when the seat was bottomed out. There are things that everyone remembers and one of those events is learning to ride a bike. The thrill of that first solo, without the supporting hand of a parent, and the crash at the end of the ride is branded in one's memory forever. To many it might be viewed as a small accomplishment, but not to a child. By the second day, jumping on one's bike and tearing off like a pro was no big deal.

My second bike was even a bigger surprise than the first. My parents were busily packing and arranging for some friends of theirs to handle the farm chores while we were away. We were going on a trip to the Rocky Mountains of Colorado. My job was to keep out of the way. I was playing with some of my toy cars on the kitchen linoleum, when our wall-mounted, crank generated phone rang: one long and two shorts. That was our call. My mother answered it, in a moment turned to me, and said that the call was for me.

She pulled over a kitchen chair so that I could reach the mouthpiece and talk into it. I held the receiver in my left hand and when I said "hello", a man's voice said, "are you Eldon Archer the son of Clyde Archer?" I said "yes", questionably. He said, "Several weeks ago you and your dad were in Brooks' grocery store and your dad bought you a sack of candy and punched out a number on a punch board; do you remember that?" I said "yes". Well this is Rom Brooks, owner of Brooks Grocery, and I just called to tell you that you have won the bicycle that was the grand prize on the punchboard.

I dropped the receiver, leaped from the chair landing on top of several pairs of shoes my mother had been polishing in preparation for our trip. An open bottle of white shoe polish tipped over and slopped white shoe polish out on the linoleum rug. When I leaped, the kitchen chair tipped over shortening my jump and left me in a tangle of shoes and polish. Sprawled on the floor, I shouted, "I won, I won, I won a new bicycle." Order was restored and my dad told Mr. Brooks that we would drive in and pick up the bike. What a day that was!

I stood on a knoll South of Norton and my recall of long forgotten experiences were continuing to compete with each other all vying for their moment to arouse my emotions. A memory pushing and shoving its way through the cells of my consciousness had never before been brought to the forefront. It was a vivid feeling of warmth and security experienced on several occasions on extremely cold winter nights as a blizzard raged its terrible vengeance on Western Kansas.

Our barn was about a hundred yards from the house. It had been built in the side of a deep draw that led to the Prairie Dog Creek. The Haymow and the door leading into it was on the same elevation as our house and garage but the entrance to the lower level of the barn on the opposite side led out into the livestock corral. It was like a walk out basement.

When it was time to milk we would enter the haymow door where our harvest of alfalfa hay was stored. Just to the left of the door was a square hole in the floor about six foot square giving us plenty of space to pitch hay down to the milking stalls below. Dad was a great believer in feeding his cows some ground corn that we called corn chop in addition to the hay. The corn chop was stored in large gunnysacks that when full held 100 pounds of ground corn. We used a one-pound Hills Brothers coffee can to measure out the corn chop for each cow and put it into a galvanized metal bucket with a bail. Whoever carried the corn chop down to the managers below inserted their arm into the bail of the bucket so they could climb the vertical ladder that descended from the haymow floor to the stalls below.

The ladder's rungs were two by four timbers nailed to vertical two by fours that were attached to the inside cement block wall of the barn. The steps were well worn over the many years of use and on one or more occasions my feet have slipped off and I have plunged to the floor below. A bucket of corn chops attached to the crook of your elbow can inflict a substantial knot on your head but fortunately I never broke any bones. We learn by our mistakes but why did I make so many mistakes?

That is not what my memory was all about. Though our barn was an important part of my early life on the farm the long forgotten experience was far more intimate. The door that closed off the lower area of the barn from the corral was an 8-foot wide door hung on steel rollers that rolled along a steel rail attached to the side of the barn. When we slid open the door the cows came into the stall area with out encouragement because they were anxious to be relieved of the heavy load of milk in their udders and they were looking forward to the hay and ground corn.

Each cow knew which stall was theirs and they put their heads through the stanchion and started munching, first the corn, then the hay. The stanchions were very low tech. One side was a permanently fixed vertical two by four timber. The other side of the stanchion was also a two by four but it pivoted on a bolt through the bottom of the board. The bolt was attached to the bottom structure of the manger. This allowed the top of the stanchion to move left and right from the neck of the cow. The open stanchion was V shaped and wide at the top. Once the cow put her head in the stanchion the timber was moved against her neck and a leather loop was slipped over the end of the vertical timber. This fastened the cow's head securely in the manager so they could not suddenly back out of the stall.

We also used kicking chains on the back legs of the cow being milked. This prevented the cow from putting her food in the milk bucket while trying to chase a pesky horse fly away from her belly where a switching tail could not reach. During fly season we always sprayed our livestock with fly spray before we started milking but that was certainly not fool proof. I have seen many a partially filled bucket of milk kicked out from between my Dad's knees by an errant cow's hoof.

Another low-tech piece of milking equipment was our milking stools. A 12-inch long four by four made up the leg of the stool and a two by six board just wide enough for one's butt was nailed to the leg for the seat. A one-legged milking stool has an advantage in that it will easily follow one's body movements as you lean in close to cow's flank or you can lean back if your aching muscles call for it.

Milking was not one of my regular chores in the early days of my youth as my fingers were too short to do an adequate job of milking. We always had two Jersey milk cows and Dad could milk both of them in the time it would have taken me to milk no more than a gallon of milk. One-day dad bought a young Jersey cow at the sale barn that was just old enough to start milking. I named her Daisy. She had very short teats so I would start milking her and then Dad would finish stripping her dry when he finished with the other two.

And now to this memory so warm and tender never before had it surfaced in my mind until this very day. In my minds eye I was sitting on my milk stool, a two-gallon pail clutched between my knees. My head was tucked in tight against Daisy warm flank, and the coal-oil lantern was flickering an aura of patterns of light into the dark shadows in and around the stalls. Outside the relentless-wind of a Kansas Blizzard was drifting snow into any shelter that it could find. The sound of squirted milk into an empty milk bucket as Dad started to milk his second cow leant to this peaceful moment. Inside the barn it was quiet and warm, compared to the raging storm outside. This haven from the storm, while man and beast were safely inside, had been deeply imprinted and tuck away nearly three quarters of a century. Why now was this memory so dear to me? Who knows? Who cares? In any case this memory stashed away so long ago was a little gem deeply protected only to be brought out at a time such as now. Letting each facet sparkle with its brilliance.

❧

THE WARMTH OF THE SUN PENETRATED DEEP INTO my back muscles mesmerizing me in these moments of tranquility. It was just such a day that my father suggested that we drive over to the sale barn and see how the previous days sale went. My Dad wanted to keep up with the local price for cattle. The community sale barn was a half-mile east of our farm and each Thursday morning they had an auction of miscellaneous items, better known as the junk sale. This was followed in the afternoon by the sale of livestock. Joe Sanderson and Earl Harrison had owned and operated the Norton Community Sale barn for many years and were very good friends of my Dad.

The sale furnished two purposes in Norton County. One, it allowed people a market to sell things at public auction for cash and secondly it offered an excuse for the farmers to come to town and socialize. Most of the women spent the day visiting and shopping in down town Norton while the men attended the sale. This gave the merchants of Norton two big days each week, sale days and Saturdays.

Dad and I attended the livestock sale quite often and he taught me to watch the various buyers around the ring. Some were commercial buyers, representing meat packing companies or stockyards located in Kansas City, Omaha, or Chicago. Other buyers were farmers in need of some livestock. The bidding was often just the touch of a hat brim; a flick of a finger, a slight nod of the head, and some of the cagey buyers might just wink at Joe Sanderson, known by everyone as Colonel Sanderson. Colonel Sanderson worked the ring keeping the livestock moving with the crack of a long buggy whip. This allowed everyone a good view of what was being bid on. Earl Harrison, the auctioneer, and the sales clerk were seated on an elevated stage several feet above the ring. Earl's continual chatter rang through the barn with a terrible din. There is no other sound like a good auctioneer and Earl was the very best. It takes a practiced ear to keep up with the lingo.

When it was apparent that the bidding had reached its peak, Earl would strike the table with a 14 inch piece of garden hose and boom out, "sold to Mr. so and so or sold to number 14" or some other number of a buyer who did not particularly want the audience to know who was in the market that particular day. The commercial buyers preferred not to be obvious with their bidding as they felt this might generate unwanted competitive biding. It was sitting on the hard wood benches at the barn that my first lessons in human psychology were learned.

I probably was not overly excited about our trip to the sale barn this particular day but wherever my Dad went I always tagged along. Little did I know, that this would be an important day in my life? I wish the cobwebs surrounding my memory were not so tenacious so that I could be more precise but I think that I was around seven or eight years old.

I STOOD ON A KNOLL SOUTH OF NORTON

The Model A coughed to a stop as Dad parked it next to a livestock pen near the office. Even before I could get out I saw the pink nose of a little pig sticking out between the boards of one of the outside pens. It was squealing and grunting and its little nose was twitching with expectation. For me, the two cutest animals were puppies and pigs. I leaped to the ground running and rushed to the pen. This scared the poor little thing and it went squealing as its little legs propelled it to the far side of the pen. The poor little critter stood there with its tiny black beady eyes surveying me. Its tiny corkscrew tail stood erect without a twitch, its short legs tensed ready to make a dash if I entered the pen. It wasn't sure whether I was friend or foe.

Dad said, "Let him be for now and when we get ready to leave maybe he will let you pet him." We started for the office when Dad's old friend Earl Harrison exited the barn. Dad and Earl had grown up together in the tiny farm town of Densmore, Kansas. They exchanged strong handshakes and told each other how good it was to see one another. A standard Kansas greeting, even if they hadn't been former classmates. My attention was still locked on the little pig and by now I could see his curly little tale wagging ever so slightly. Maybe that crazy little kid was all right after all. Earl Harrison said to Dad, "in all the years we have operated this sale barn we have never had a buyer leave any animal here after their purchase. I don't understand how they missed that pig after the sow and her brood were loaded, but they did." "I was just in the office trying to find out who bought the sow and pigs but we had several lots like that yesterday and I don't know who that pig belongs to."

Dad said, "I'll tell you what I'll do, Earl, I'll give you a dollar for the pig and if you find the owner they can come over to our place and get it. If not then the pig belongs to

Eldon." "It's a deal said Earl." They shook on it and a new dimension of my life began. My father constantly surprising me but I remember this episode as one of the best. The pig was not nearly as excited about this deal as I was. It took the three of us to finally corner the squealing little devil and put him in a cardboard box and tie down the lid with binder twine. On the way home Dad said, "son this is your first farm animal to own and raise. I expect you to be responsible for him and when he is ready for market, the money will be yours." Private enterprise was a phrase totally foreign to me then, but that was my beginning in the world of commerce.

The Model A had not even been braked to a stop when I hit the ground running toward the house to share the good news with my Mother and Sister. From that day on I looked after that pig with the greatest of care. What a thrill I had with the pride of ownership and the relationship I developed with that pig. It was an immediate bonding and from day one he loved to have his back scratched. He especially liked to have his head scratched between his ears. I can hear today the soft grunts of contentment echoing through the halls of my memory.

When his bristles became as thick as the teeth on a comb, I used a corncob to curry him. Sometime it would take thirty minutes or more to brush off the dried mud from his back and sides after he had wallowed in the perpetual mud hole we kept in the corner of the coral. This was important for all of our hogs to keep cool. and to coat themselves with mud so they did not sunburn. Pig, as we called him, was all white and below his bristles his skin was pink and very tender.

One day my Dad told me that it was time to sell my investment. I knew from the beginning that this day would come but it was a bittersweet experience. I was anxious to have a good sum of money but I would sure miss this hog. I did not go to the sale with Dad, fortunately I was attending school. If I had been able to go I might have cried and that would have been totally unacceptable to me.

I could hardly believe it when I got home from school and Dad handed me a check made payable to Eldon Archer for forty-one dollars. That was a fortune. My young mind, calculated that a one-dollar investment had reaped a forty-dollar profit. What I failed to consider was that my folks had paid for the corn chop and bran that I mixed with our excess cow's milk to make a slop that I fed to a pig rearing it into a marketable hog.

Stepping in to the world of high finance had another important lesson attached. That was what to do with forty-one dollars. This was during the heart of the depression and banks were paying nothing in interest on money that was on deposit. Dad explained to me that the Federal Government had through the Postal System established a savings plan called Postal Savings. If I deposited this fortune of mine in a Postal Savings account I would get 1% interest added to my deposit. It was another very important lesson taught to me by my parents.

I STOOD ON A KNOLL SOUTH OF NORTON, the grass now dry and the sun an hour plus into its arc of travel. Its warming rays penetrating my shirt had smoothed the goose bumps that had prickled my skin as memories flooded my mind and the tears of joy moistened my eyes. The quiet, magical moment had abruptly ended. Why had I been so obsessed to come, I still do not know? Maybe it was my way of giving thanks. Maybe I needed to have these moments with God to glimpse the past. Maybe it was a way of honoring my parents, physically gone, yet so near to me. Whatever the reason, I am thankful. Time is a fleeting thing, an asset not to be wasted. Opportunities come and go. I wonder if I will every return for a second view from this little knoll just South of Norton.

CPSIA information can be obtained
at www.ICGtesting.com
Printed in the USA
BVOW03s1102101017
497241BV00001B/32/P